CULTURE

THE NEW SCIENCE SERIES

Edited by C. K. OGDEN

Myth in Primitive Psychology
Bronislaw Malinowski, Ph.D., D.Sc.

Science and Poetry   I. A. Richards

Fatalism or Freedom   C. Judson Herrick, M.S., Ph.D.

A Short Outline of Comparative Psychology
C. J. Warden, Ph.D.

Types of Mind and Body
E. Miller, M.A. (Cantab.), M.B., M.R.C.S.

The Father in Primitive Psychology
Bronislaw Malinowski, Ph.D., D.Sc.

The Standardization of Error
Vilhjalmur Stefansson, M.A., LL.D.

Economics and Human Behavior
P. Sargant Florence, Ph.D.

Culture   G. Elliott Smith, D.Sc.; Bronislaw Malinowski, Ph.D., D.Sc.; Herbert J. Spinden,
Ph.D.; Alexander Goldenweiser, Ph.D.

Other Volumes in Preparation

Each Volume, $1.00

W · W · NORTON & COMPANY, INC.
70 FIFTH AVENUE   *NEW YORK*

CULTURE

The Diffusion Controversy

BY

G. ELLIOTT SMITH, D.Sc.
BRONISLAW MALINOWSKI, D.Sc.
HERBERT J. SPINDEN, Ph.D.
ALEX. GOLDENWEISER, Ph.D.

NEW YORK
W·W·NORTON & COMPANY, INC.
Publishers

PRINTED IN THE UNITED STATES OF AMERICA

FOR THE PUBLISHERS BY THE VAN REES PRESS

CONTENTS

	PAGE
THE DIFFUSION OF CULTURE . *G. Elliot Smith*	9
THE LIFE OF CULTURE . . *Bronislaw Malinowski*	26
THE PROSAIC VS. THE ROMANTIC SCHOOL IN ANTHROPOLOGY . *Herbert J. Spinden*	47
THE DIFFUSION CONTROVERSY . *Alexander Goldenweiser*	99

CULTURE

THE DIFFUSION OF CULTURE

By G. ELLIOT SMITH
Professor of Anatomy in the University of London

AT the present time among students of mankind there are two conflicting views as to the process that has played the most essential part in the history of civilization. One, the theory maintained by the vast majority of anthropologists to-day, is that in any community civilization can and did grow up and develop quite independently of similar events happening elsewhere in the world. This involves a further consideration. For if any community can of its own initiative create a civilization, a more difficult problem has to be solved: why it acquires a multitude of features in its arts and crafts, customs, and beliefs that present a striking similarity to those of other communities, when all considerations of contact or prompting directly or indirectly are excluded. The other group of anthropologists believes that civilization has been developing during the whole of its history in very much the same way that we know it to be doing at the present time, and in fact during the whole period of which we have any written record. We know in the case of every modern invention, that it was made in one definite place and became diffused over a wider and wider area until everyone in any part of the world who is making use of this particular invention is indebted directly or indirectly to one man in one particular place who was originally responsible for initiating the process.

Take, for example, the history of the wooden match. For countless thousands of years men have been devising and using different means of producing fire. During the latter part of the eighteenth and early part of the nineteenth centuries, a series of modifications and simplifications of one particular method developed, until eventually one man made the discovery that he could put upon the end of a strip of wood a chemical mixture that under the influence of friction would give rise to fire. Now although at the present day this seems to be a perfectly simple and obvious procedure, we know that it took countless centuries to arrive at the result, and that eventually one individual brought it to realization. We know, of course, as an historical fact that this invention has spread throughout the world from one particular spot. But if some European traveler who was unaware of this fact was roaming in a part of the world where no white man had ever been before, and found there a wooden match, he would inevitably conclude that the match afforded certain evidence of contact, direct or indirect, with someone who had benefited by the English invention. If, however, he were not a mere man-in-the-street, but an ethnologist faithful to the orthodox theory of his creed, he would have to assume that so obvious a mechanism must have been invented independently by the uncultured people of the country where he had picked up the match.

If, on the other hand, he belonged to what our opponents call the "Diffusionist School" of anthropology, he would assume (as every intelligent man-in-the-street would unhesitatingly do, whether he was familiar with the history of the wooden match or not) that the match itself provided unequivocal evidence of diffusion of culture. He would not entertain any doubt that it had reached the place where it was found either directly from the home of its invention, or from some community that had learned the art of making matches directly or indirectly from it. Nor would this conclusion be affected even if the finder of the match could tell at a glance whether the particular match was made in Sweden or Japan, for the match-makers of these two countries had had the art handed down to them from the original inventor who belonged to neither of these countries. What we of the Diffusionist School assume is that the processes of the origin, development, and spread of any invention in the time before written records were made, followed the same sort of course we know to have happened in the case of the match. These are recorded in the written histories of the various inventions and the struggles of the pioneers to get their achievements recognized and adopted. But anyone can see and study the same processes happening round him at the present time in the community in which he lives.

It is utterly unjustifiable to assume, as modern ethnological theories implicitly do, that human behaviour was totally different before writing was devised. There is not a scrap of evidence to suggest that our unliterary predecessors had a remarkable aptitude for invention far transcending that of modern man. Nor again is there anything to justify the even more reckless assumption that this imaginary aptitude found expression in a stereotyped form in every place where ancient civilization developed.

For example, there is no natural reason for attaching the tremendous economic and religious significance to gold, which is an arbitrary enhancement of its real qualities. The fact that almost every early civilization did assign to this soft and relatively useless metal a fantastic and irrelevant value is surely the strongest possible evidence of the influence of Egypt, in which a peculiar set of fortuitous circumstances was responsible for creating the fictitious attributes assigned to the metal.

DIFFUSION OF CULTURE

One might take up one after another of the thousands of ingredients that go to the making of civilization, ancient or modern, and show in each case the complexity of the set of circumstances, in which chance played an obstrusive part, involved in every invention. Each of them originated in one place and from there became diffused abroad, the complex tissue of civilization itself no less than the individual threads of which it is woven.

Turning to the consideration of the general question, no historian at the present day refuses to admit that Europe is indebted for the original inspiration of her civilization to Greece and to Rome, and that Rome in her turn derived much of her culture from Greece. Modern archaeological research has shown that Greece derived much of her own civilization from Crete and Asia Minor, and that both of these countries were in turn indebted to the older civilization of

[15]

Egypt for their cultural equipment. This much is admitted by the leading archaeologists who have been working in Crete. At the present time there is a difference of opinion as to whether Egypt or Mesopotamia was the pioneer in civilization; but among modern scholars the trend is strongly toward the view that whether Egypt was indebted to Mesopotamia, or Mesopotamia to Egypt, there was intimate contact between the two, and that one borrowed the essential elements of its civilization from the other.

This claim for diffusion is confidently made even by some of the most outspoken opponents of the theory of diffusion—a typical illustration of the inconsistency that runs through these discussions. The view is widely held amongst archaeologists that Babylonian civilization, or rather its predecessor, that of Sumer, is more ancient than that of Egypt. This is an amazing inference. For it is admitted, even by those now excavating in Mesopotamia, that the earliest Sumerian remains cannot be proved to be older than 3000 B.C. Yet, even if we accept the minimum dating of Egyptian history, the First Dynasty was flourishing on the banks of the Nile three centuries before then, and even so it followed a predynastic phase of development of several—perhaps as many as ten—centuries, which affords a full and adequate explanation of the form that Egyptian civilization had assumed in 3300 B.C.

I need not discuss this matter further here. Professor George A. Reisner of Harvard University has demonstrated in the most conclusive manner that Egyptian civilization was actually fashioned in the Nile Valley. As there can be no doubt of the genetic connection between the earliest civilizations of Egypt, Sumer, and Elam, one must assume that these Asiatic centres must have derived their cultural capital

from Egypt, where civilization had
been developing for five, or more
probably ten, centuries before culture
appeared suddenly and fully developed
in Elam and Sumer. The evidence
in substantiation of these claims I have
set forth in the article "Anthropology"
in the supplementary volumes of the
Encyclopaedia Britannica (1922).

The excavations of Professor Pum-
pelly at Anau in Turkestan have re-
vealed the influence of Sumer and
Elam, in the country east of the Cas-
pian, which represents a step in the
diffusion right up into the heart of
Siberia and into the Shensi Province
in China. The recent discoveries by
M. J. G. Andersson of early settle-
ments in northern China (the Provinces of Honan and Fengtien) established even more exactly the affinities
of the original culture of China to
that of Anau, Elam, Sumer, and other
centres in western Asia. These people
in the Far East were making arrow-

heads of chalcedony and other flint-like stones, also other stone implements, rings of stone and shell, beads, pottery (both monochrome and painted), and even small figurines, all revealing clear and unmistakable indications of diffusion of culture from Mesopotamia.

The influence of Mesopotamia upon India in the third millennium is equally definite. There was a spread by land from Turkestan as well as from Persia, from the ancient civilization of Elam into the valley of the Indus. The recent discoveries announced by Sir John Marshall have established this fact beyond any doubt. At the same time or possibly at an even earlier period western culture was being brought into southern India by early mariners sailing in ships conforming in every respect to the peculiar type of vessel invented originally for navigation on the Nile in the Pyramid Age.

CULTURE

No one questions the dominant influence of India in inspiring the earliest civilization of Indo-China and of the islands of the Malay Archipelago. The early culture of the islands of the Pacific could have come only from the southeastern corner of Asia and the West. The debt of Africa to Egypt is beyond question. Hence one can demonstrate with an enormously rich mass of evidence the spread of civilization throughout the Old World from one centre, which must clearly have been in the valley of the Nile. The distinctive form and outlook of the world's civilization were determined by the methods of early agriculture, based upon the experience of a gentle and beneficent river like the Nile. The fact that so much of early belief was inspired by the essentially Egyptian practice of mummification would alone provide adequate proof that Egypt was the home of the earliest civilization. But the whole body of evidence corroborates this view. Throughout the world the earliest types of sea-going ship provide unmistakable demonstration of the inspiration of Egyptian methods of shipbuilding, which is itself both a corroboration of the general inference and also a demonstration of the means by which this wide diffusion was brought about.

A very curious argument has repeatedly been put to me verbally. But fortunately Mr. Enthoven has recently used it in print (in the issue of *Folk-Lore* for September, 1925, p. 224). If, he argues, it be admitted that the Egyptians without any outside help invented irrigation, why couldn't the peoples of India have done the same thing? This plausible line of argument is purely scholastic. What we have to do is to find an explanation of the established facts rather than speculate on what could or ought to happen. The very peculiar methods of agriculture used in the earliest times were determined by conditions peculiar to the Nile Valley, as Professor Cherry has made abundantly clear, and these methods were not adapted to Indian conditions until many centuries later.

There remains the problem of early American civilization. Did the Pre-Columbian civilization grow up in Mexico, Central America, and Peru, quite independently of what had happened during the preceding centuries in the Old World, or did diffusion of the arbitrary compound of customs and beliefs extend beyond the Old World to the New and provide the stimulus for the momentous events that began to take place there at about the beginning of the Christian Era? In Central America, Mexico, and Peru civilization made its appearance quite suddenly, and in a fully developed form. But there is another fact to be explained: it conformed in almost every respect to the distinctive type of civilization (admittedly a very peculiar one) that was flourishing in the southeastern corner of Asia at the time when it made its appearance in Central America. The type of pyramid found in America was also the dominant feature of the architecture of Cambodia and Java during the same centuries. The same system of beliefs and customs, the same distinctive features of its architecture, in fact a whole series of arts and crafts, customs and beliefs, were suddenly introduced into the New World, which seem to bear unmistakable evidence of their Asiatic origin. Moreover, the only additions that were made to these customs in their transit across the Pacific were features distinctive of Melanesian and Polynesian practices. Instead of detracting from the cogency of the identity, these trivial additions afford striking corroboration, not only of the original source of the inspiration, but also of the road taken by the ancient mariners who were responsible for the introduction into the New World of the germs of its distinctive civilization. It is an altogether incredible supposition that the Polynesian sailors who searched many thousands of miles in the Pacific with such thoroughness as not to miss even the minutest islets were not repeatedly landing on the shores of America for ten centuries and more. How could the people who found Hawaii, Easter Island, and New Zealand have failed to discover the vast continent stretching from pole to pole?

In his memoir on the *Copper and Bronze Ages in South America* Baron Nordenskiold has recently called attention to the similarities of metal-work in Peru and in the Old World. Copper axes similar to those found in Cambodia, Laos, Burma, the Malay Peninsula, the Malay Archipelago, Tonkin, Yunnan, and elsewhere in China have been found in Peru. The T-shaped axes from Peru are said to be precisely similar to those made in Ancient Egypt. Many other copper objects, such as tweezers, barbless fish-hooks, needles, hoe-blades, and certain types of hoes, still further emphasize the significance of these similarities. But it is not merely the form, but also the technical procedures for making these metal utensils that establish the cultural connection. The method of casting known as *cire perdue* was common both to the Old and the New Worlds, as also the technique of gilding and silvering. The truth of any scientific theory that cannot be tested by direct experiment can be established only by examining newly discovered evidence and deciding whether or not it conforms to the principles laid down.

THE LIFE OF CULTURE

By Bronislaw Malinowski

Reader in Anthropology at the London School of Economics

ANTHROPOLOGY, the Science of Man and of his Culture, has for the most part tried to evade live issues and the problems of life: it has tried to shelter behind the Chinese Wall of mere antiquarian curiosity. In all humanistic studies there is a strong temptation to play about with dead remains instead of grappling with actualities; to affect a so-called "purely academic" interest in theory, to abstain from testing doctrines in the crucible of practical reality.

The anthropologist of the past has felt safe in spinning his hypotheses about what did happen when Man tried to evolve from the Pithecanthropos Erectus, or else, tired of inventing "origins" and "developments," he began to manufacture out of his inner consciousness various "histories" and "diffusions." This latter line of approach is now fashionable, and a number of anthropologists of the day are busy reconstructing the influence of Egyptian culture on Central America; they quarrel as to whether all civilization started in Mesopotamia, Atlantis, or Pamir. This historical or diffusionist trend is now being advertised as the "revolutionary" or "modern" school of anthropology, though in reality it is as old as the Ten Lost Tribes fallacy. The hypothesis of the origins of all culture in Egypt, for instance, was invented long ago by a German scholar, Eduard Braun, though it received little "diffusion" at that time.

Those who support the extreme diffusionist view are wont to frame the problem in a singularly insidious manner, inquiring as to whether diffusion or independent invention had been the dominant factor in progress. As usually happens in the perpetration of scientific fallacies, the error has been introduced into the framing of the question. Hence we are tempted at first sight to jump to the erroneous answer. The correct reply to the above question, however, must insist that the very opposition, sharp and precise though it appears, between diffusion and invention, is really misleading.

Let us inquire, then, what precisely an "invention" is. In the case of every modern invention, we know that it is invariably made and re-made time after time in different places, by different men along slightly different roads, independently of one another. It is enough to mention the famous disputes about the discovery of the infinitesimal calculus, the steam engine, the telephone, the turbine, the wireless; the endless priority wrangles in science; the difficulties of establishing rights to a patent; and so on. The fact is that each invention is arrived at piece-meal, by infinitely many, infinitely small steps, a process in which it is impossible to assign a precise share to any one worker or still less to connect a definite object and a definite idea with a single contribution. In the wireless, for instance, the man to whom the invention is popularly ascribed has little more than commercialized the already existing practical appliances. The real work can be traced back through Righi, Braun, Hertz, Clerk-Maxwell, Faraday, Ampère, and so on back to Galvani and Galileo. But these are only the summits—illuminated by the flash-light of sensational coincidence and the lime-light of success as well as by the elevation of their genius. The real pathway of ideas and achievements goes through hundreds and thousands of humbler workers and laboratory mechanics, the mathematicians and engineers who jointly make the final success possible. Thus the invention of the wireless can be treated as a single and singular event and ascribed to one man or another only after its nature has been completely misconceived. This is quite legitimate from the point of view of the patent office, but quite erroneous for the science of culture.

Every cultural achievement is due to a process or growth in which diffusion and invention have equal shares. As independent entities, neither invention nor diffusion ever takes place in the sense that you could either spontaneously generate an idea or pour it out from one head into another. Diffusion and invention are always mixed, always inseparable.

If it is impossible to speak of either of these phenomena in isolation or as absolute categories within the same culture, the definition becomes especially fallacious when we deal with the contact of different cultures. Just because no idea and no object can exist in isolation from its cultural context, it is impossible to sever mechanically an item from one culture and place it in another. The process is always one of adaptation in which the receiving culture has to re-evolve the idea, custom, or institution which it adopts; and it can be said without exaggeration that diffusion is a partial evolution, though the contrary is not true.

A puerile example is sometimes used by those who believe that culture can be contracted only by contagion and that man is merely an imitative monkey. We are asked whether a wooden match found in use among a Negro, Pigmy, or Papuan tribe has been invented by them or diffused to them. The answer is, *neither*. A wooden match, as I have found it in use in Papua and in Melanesia, among the Australian aborigines and the North

American Indians, is not a part of the culture of these natives. It has been mechanically imported and supplied to them by the trader. I have watched Melanesian natives time after time producing fire by friction when, during the War, there was a difficulty in obtaining matches. The match had never been part of their culture. They could neither produce nor procure it. It has to be put into their hands by another society which is in contact with them and which has never succeeded in "diffusing" its chemistry, physics, and engineering into the Melanesian culture. We might quite as well ask whether a baby has invented the golden watch which has been put into its hands and take the denial as a dialectical triumph. I have myself seen the savage invent independently the counterpart of a wooden match by putting some kerosene on the end of a rubbing stick to make it flare up more easily, so that even this apparently obvious example of the impossibility of independent invention is not adequate.

Archæology and history furnish us with a number of definite instances in which a type of mechanical contrivance, an art, or a social institution, can be shown to have evolved independently in different cultures. Take music, for instance, which produces parallel effects as it satisfies parallel cravings, but has such a distinctly different imprint among the Mongolian, Semitic, Melanesian, Papuan, and Caucasian races that it cannot be "diffused" even under pressure, as is shown by the inability of another race to grasp our melodies, and vice versa. The existence in social organization, in religion, in language, and in economics of cultural contrivances which satisfy the same need, which are thus functionally akin, and which yet bear an entirely different physiognomy and are carried out by entirely different mechanisms, spells all over the surface of human culture the assertion of independent origins. The compass, the art of writing, chemistry, the calendar —all were independently invented, as is known to archæologists. Paper was made of papyrus in Egypt, of rags in China, of another material in Mexico. It is identical only in its function. The technique of production, the material or way of using it, had to be independently invented.

Extreme diffusionism appears on closer analysis as futile and fallacious as the belief that every culture follows an independent course of evolution. The remedy for anthropology lies not in conjuring up one conjecture in the place of another, but in giving the science of man a foundation of real fact open to observation, in making it bear upon the practical and vital issues of to-day. What are the problems in which it can be made practically useful and what are the methods by which it can be made, if not experimental, at least empirical?

It is obviously impossible to place an empire under glass, to treat a savage chief or a modern politician as the biologist treats his guinea-pig. The anthropologist is not even allowed to observe long stretches of human history, while savages have no written records and have left few monuments. For all this, however, the anthropologist is compensated by the wide range of his material, by the variety of cultures from the crudest Stone Age to the highest flights of modern civilization.

But the comparative method is beset with many pitfalls. One of these has been the simple evolutionary assumption by which all variations were assigned to differences in level and all similarities to the same universal sequence of evolutionary stages. Development thus was regarded as a metaphysical fatality driving man to some sort of Hegelian self-realization. Not less fatalistic, however, is the view which makes culture shoot up in one place as a glorious and miraculous accident, and thence be mechanically transported all over the globe.

To the modern anthropologist trained in the field, culture, whether savage or civilized, is not a heap of trinkets which can be peddled about across oceans and round continents. Living among one savage tribe after another, the anthropological field-worker becomes convinced that culture is something which is constantly at work, which is there for the satisfaction of elementary human needs, which in turn creates new wants and provides means for their fulfilment.

Man, making a generous allowance for Tennessee, has evolved from the animal; there is no necessity to believe, with the psychoanalyst, that all civilization is but a roundabout satisfaction of the sexual instinct, in order to realize that a wide domain—the organization of the family, the customs of courtship and mating, domestic arrangements, the clan, exogamy, and a part of human morals—can only be properly accounted for as an expression of the human biological need for propagation and the cultural need for educating each generation. Culture creates new forms of love-making, of marriage, of family life, but they are all directly correlated with the biological arrangements by which courtship, mating, and family life are regulated in the state of nature.

Again, though the historical materialists are no doubt mistaken in telling us that mankind advances on its belly, the need for nutrition, as well as the appetites, instincts, and tendencies which it governs, plays an enormous part in primitive and in higher cultures. The psychology of taking meals in common, of festive eating, of nutrition rites, totemic feasts, and acts of communion; the sacramental value of accumulated food and its rôle in primitive religion; the ramification of the economical aspect in the magical and religious—all this cannot be understood if we forget that man is an omnivorous animal, and that eating under conditions of culture is not merely an absorption of food, but a communal bond, a sacrament, and a source of social, artistic, and religious values.

Now nutrition and sex drive man to the search for food and companionship, to hunting, fishing, and scouring his district; and thus they compel him to master his surroundings, to exploit his territory, and to conquer its natural resources; they also compel him to live a communal life. In all this man's success is dependent upon his material outfit in implements, weapons, and constructions, upon the perfection of his knowledge, and on the degree of his social organization.

But here in the very act of bestowing

her blessings, culture heaps up burdens and creates difficulties. The fruit of knowledge is a dangerous thing, and in giving man forethought, culture gives him also the terrors and pangs of despondency; it makes him probe into his own destiny, and ponder over the ultimate things of human existence. Belief in immortality, early ideas of spirit gods and beneficent favours, give man comfort and dispel his early misgivings. Again since man is to adventure in pursuits for which he is not equipped instinctively—to move through water, jungle, and desert, to invade and conquer cold, arid, and tropical places— culture has to provide man with a mental force which carries him across the gaps in instinctive endowment. The confidence in his own powers of controlling his environment by spell and rite are given to man in magic.

And here we have gained a very important insight into the nature of primitive ritual and belief. The value of so-called savage "superstition" and the essence of primitive belief is to be found in the confidence which magical rite gives man in forgetting difficulties and in bridging over gaps in which he is forsaken by his knowledge and technical abilities. Primitive religion, again, by assuring man of his immortality, by revealing to him the existence of a benevolent providence, by guiding him sacramentally through the crises of life, gives him the metaphysical comfort without which life becomes an intolerable burden to a being endowed with forethought, knowledge, and sentiment. Primitive religion thus appears as a more important and more valuable aspect of savage culture.

The functional analysis makes us regard culture primarily as an outfit which gives man the mastery of his environment, allows him to maintain the species, the integrity of the individual, and the cohesion of his tribe. The practical value of such a theory is that it teaches us the relative importance of various customs, how they dovetail into each other, how they have to be handled by missionaries, colonial authorities, and those who economically have to exploit savage trade and savage labour.

The functional view obviously does not dispose of a sound and limited evolutionary conception of culture, though it discourages any hope of giving an exact reconstruction of human development. It strengthens our conviction that the denial of evolution by pseudo-religious and pseudo-scientific fundamentalists is but a wilful misapprehension. Moreover, the functional method in no way denies or minimizes diffusion, its influence on the course of evolution, the importance of tracing its probable routes. But it teaches us that diffusion never takes place in the form of mere mechanical transmission. Whenever one culture "borrows" from another, it always transforms and readapts the objects or customs borrowed. The idea, institution, or contrivance has to be placed within a new cultural milieu, fitted into it, and assimilated to the receiving civilization. In this process of readaptation the form and function, often the very nature, of the object or idea is deeply modified—it has to be, in short, reinvented. Diffusion is but a modified invention, exactly as every invention is a partial borrowing. What is really important to the anthropologist is the nature of the cultural process which is mixed borrowing and invention, and the study of its mechanism and its general laws. To explain away one culture as a mere result of "diffusion" is as misleading as to account for it by an imaginary trend of universal evolution.

No culture is a simple copy of any other. No historian of present-day European culture would dare assign it to any one original source. He knows perfectly well that we have borrowed from everywhere, from ancient Greece as well as China and Japan, from India and from aboriginal America, and that out of the mixture we have evolved an entirely independent and homogeneous culture. Modern archaeology absolutely and explicitly repudiates the suggestion that Asiatic, Cretan, or Aegean civilization is any more indebted to Egypt than Egypt is to any of the surrounding civilizations. Authorities such as Sir Flinders Petrie, the greatest British Egyptologist, as well as Professor J. L. Myers of Oxford and Sir Arthur Evans, have all laughed to scorn the suggestion that Egypt has been even to a limited degree the source of civilized life. Always subject to natural law, man was in his development bound to strike on a number of contrivances and ideas which were essentially similar.

Take, for instance, gold. To anyone ignorant of physics, chemistry, and cultural technique there might appear something mystical about the attraction which gold has for primitive man, for the modern prospector, and for the demi-mondaine. Yet a minute's reflection shows that a similar attraction is exercised by silver, a slightly smaller one by copper, and that iron is for certain native tribes, notably African, almost as seductive as the nobler metals. Again, gold and silver are the only metals found extensively in a native condition, and gold is the more malleable of the two. It is absurd to speak of it as a "soft and relatively useless metal," and to regard its value as arbitrary, if we remember that it is an indispensable substance in modern technique where the dentist, the fountain-pen manufacturer, the optician, and the industrial chemist are prepared to pay high prices for it apart from its value as means of exchange. Even clearer is the case of other materials, the stone for primitive axes, the hard wood for implements, large stones employed for building, and so on. Or are we to suppose that the use of fire for warmth and cooking, of water for drinking and irrigation, or air for breathing is each a cultural invention once made in Egypt and thence diffused? The question might appear absurd had it not been seriously put forward that the use of water for irrigation, of large stones for building, of gold for practical and decorative uses, is due to one single influence diffused all over the world.

In conclusion then: it has been maintained by the diffusionists that the one centre of original invention was Egypt, that this civilization was diffused into the Mediterranean basin, and into western Asia, India, China, and further across the Pacific, even into America; and that the higher cultures are copies of the Egyptian prototype.

To this we reply that every aspect of culture—the implements and arts, social organization, law, magic, and religion—correspond to a specific need of human nature, to the local environment, and to the general character of a given civilization. Both from the latest technical achievements and from ancient history numerous examples can be given of independent parallel inventions.

Diffusion never takes place: it is always a readaptation, a truly creative process, in which external influence is remoulded by inventive genius. The culture of Egypt is no older than that of China, Mesopotamia, or India, and it took as much from its neighbours as it gave. Civilization is fortunately not a disease—not always at least—and the immunity of most people to culture is notorious: *culture is not contagious!* It has neither been invented nor diffused, but imposed by the natural conditions which drive man upon the path of progress with inexorable determinism.

THE PROSAIC VS. THE ROMANTIC SCHOOL IN ANTHROPOLOGY

By Herbert J. Spinden

Peabody Museum, Harvard University

Does man, at large, think or merely remember? This query strikes the bed-rock logic which distinguishes the prosaic from the romantic schools of anthropology.

For the prosaic school insists that man does think and that separate societies of human beings make similar but not necessarily uniform inductions and deductions from experience and are thus capable of solving independently about the same problems of life in about the same way. Moreover, the prosaic school insists that there are important mechanical factors, both within and without the body of man, which lead to frequent conformities in his manifold thoughts whether these are expressed in words, or tools, or objects of beauty, or ceremonies, or the forms of government. Human institutions, in the words of Tylor, belong in "series substantially the same over the globe." There are common psychic trends if not complete psychic unity among all the races of mankind. Similar experiences are everywhere producing similar results in handicraft and statecraft. The prosaic school of anthropology accepts the possibility of independent invention—of thoughts finding expression over and over again —and sees no need for straining historical evidence beyond the elastic limit to account for the dissemination of certain cultural traits around the world.

The romantic school, on the other hand, sees in cultural similarities the almost certain proofs of dissemination from a favoured intellectual source even though ages and oceans intervene. The members of this school picture the great mass of humanity as devoid of inventive ability but possessed of an extremely retentive memory. Ancient transmissions and inoculations, of which history furnishes not the slightest direct evidence, are invoked as a logical necessity where there is any detail to be exploited as a surviving strain. But the romanticists agree with each other only in the hypothetical need of contacts between distant peoples and they differ grotesquely from each other as to the ways and means of obtaining these contacts. Their numerous special theses force them to invent variegated, stranger-than-fiction explanations. Only outstanding hypotheses can be reviewed.

THE ROUND OF ROMANTIC THEORIES

America with her teeming nations had no sooner been discovered by Euro-

peans than writers of romantic mood
began to find similarities in culture to
the Old World and to explain them
by miraculous immigrations from a
single fountain head of all good things.
In those days the complexion of ancient history was biblical and there
was a rush to discover among American
Indians a knowledge of Adam and Eve,
the Tower of Babel, Noah's Ark upon
the Flood, the dry-shod crossing of the
Red Sea, the Crucifixion of Christ and
the subsequent worship of the Cross
with much impedimenta of Christian-
ity. Quetzalcoatl, a Toltec monarch
who died in 1208 A.D., was confidently
identified with St. Thomas, while the
American aborigines became the Ten
Lost Tribes of Israel. This pattern
was well set before 1600 A.D. among
Spanish churchmen, yet it inspired
Lord Kingsborough to waste his for-
tune in a monumental publication given
to the world between 1831 and 1848.
Long before this great work ap-

peared, however, the Phœnicians had been glorified at the cost of their Semitic brothers. Because they had crept along shore to the Scilly Islands and even to the Canaries, it was deemed probable that they also crossed the broad Atlantic. Next Modoc with his Welshmen and St. Brandon with his Irishmen were found to have left home and since they did not return it was believed that they had reached America. When George Catlin reached the Mandans on the upper Missouri he saw many resemblances between this people and the Welsh, which vanished into thin air under scientific examination.

Egypt was not neglected in sundry speculations, and China came into her own as a proposed source of the Central American civilization by writers improving on curious hints of Humboldt, who merely flirted with the idea. John Ranking in 1823 wrote his *Historical Researches on the Conquest of*

[51]

Peru, Mexico, Bogota, Natchez and Talomeco in the Thirteenth Century by the Mongols, Accompanied with Elephants. The bones of the mammoth and the mastodon proved his case, although he asserted that in his time a few Chinese elephants were still running wild about Bogota. The existence of jade in America gave rise to the jade theory which also involved China. Happily now this is dissipated by chemical analyses which distinguish the oriental from the occidental stones. Other writers dabbled with zodiacs of Assyrian, Hindoo or Chinese types, and by this astrology explained the Central American calendar.

Perhaps the most daring group of romantic writers seized upon a Greek fable referring vaguely to the Canary Islands, if to any real location. These pulled up a great continent out of 30,000 feet of ocean, as Maui, the Maori god, pulled up New Zealand on his fishing line. But the Lost At-

lantis sank again after permitting the
Mayas to walk dry shod to Africa for
the purpose of founding Egypt, if Le
Plongeon is to be believed, while Ig-
nacius Donnelly would have the young
Greeks planting their dynamic sym-
metries in Mexico by the reverse route.
Louis Spence within a year or two has
revived this watery highway, partly by
picturing Quetzalcoatl as none other
than the world-weary Atlas.

Today we find two tumultuous theories bearing down on ancient America
from diametrically opposite directions,
the one sponsored by Leo Wiener and
the other by G. Elliot Smith.

Professor Wiener solves the riddle
of old American civilizations with an
Arabico-Mendingo lexicon and derives
everything of importance in the New
World from the highly civilized coasts
of Gambia and Sierra Leone. From
brightest Africa came the principal
American food plants, the Mayan
calendar and the Mexican religion.

He has accomplished this end by making vague and caliginous comparisons with outlandish words, after finding the "single alif" of Omar that is the key to everything. The full splendor of his disarticulation is demonstrated in several books. One, freshly off the press, has 110 colored plates and 16 plates in black and white, a veritable monument to misguided enthusiasm. In this highly colored thesaurus numerous American names are neatly warped to African sources, but the illustrations coming from Mexican and Mayan books find no parallels in Africa. It may be added that Professor Wiener swarms his Negroes across the Atlantic in no less than fifty voyages before Columbus. He refuses to give Poor Lo even the honour of knowing tobacco and recognizes no specimens of tobacco pipes as truly archæological. He accounts for the fine cotton cloth of Peru on the ground that bodies were dug up and re-clothed in post-Spanish times.

PROSAIC VS. ROMANTIC

ROMANTIC ANTHROPOLOGY IN GERMANY AND ENGLAND

Lowie, in his treatise on Social Anthropology in the new section of the Encyclopædia Britannica mentions two "diffusionist" or romantic groups whose major operations have been conducted across the Pacific. They use different methods but an indifferent logic.

The first of these diffusionist groups is German, with F. Graebner and W. Schmidt as the outstanding leaders and the second is English with H. R. Rivers (now dead and worthy of better remembrances for his early work), G. Elliot Smith and W. J. Perry directing the offensive. Each team ignores the possibility of independent civilization and believes, to quote Lowie, that "similarities are *ipso facto* evidence of transmission, and the proof is perfect when not merely single traits but complexes recur—megalithic monuments *and* a sun colt, conical roofs *and* a solar mythology, rectangular huts *and* a division into matrilinear descent." But if recapitulating thought is not possible among men, then memory must be invoked to preserve the historical continuities, as various quaint ideas, distributed by imaginary migrations, are found to survive in the four quarters of the globe.

Comparative calm settled over anthropological doctrine in the first ten years of the twentieth century following the overthrow of those romanticists who had trailed civilization by the swastika and the ring-and-cross symbol. Then the world was startled by the announcement of Graebner that the costumes of the "devil dancers" on the Amazon and Orinoco were historically connected with those of the Dukduk ceremony in the Bismarck Archipelago. This proof, affecting primitive peoples of different race and language, separated by half the circumference of the world, consisted in nothing more significant in human affairs than over-size conical hats with fringes on the rim. These hats were large enough nearly to conceal the body of the wearer and therefore to serve as complete costumes.

The general argument of the diffusive Germans, built on raw facts like the above, was that three "primary" cultures arose from the rock-bottom simplicity of nomadic hunters. One of these was strongly feminist, due to women's invention of agriculture, and its religious and artistic expressions were concerned with female deities and lunar mythology. A second was masculine in temperament and had its birth in the perfection of manly arts and was devoted to patrilinear descent, totemism, male deities and solar myths. A third primary culture emerged after the domestication of animals and was developed by pastoral nomads. The later course of history was a mingling of germ plasm from these first sources of social life.

The modern English diffusionists derive everything worth while from a so-called archaic civilization which had its origin in Egypt or thereabouts. Numerous ideas were planted in all parts of the world by adventurous bands who departed from this cradle of original thought in search of gold, pearls and what-not. Mr. H. G. Wells, with truly dramatic instinct, placed the origin of this civilization on the present bottom of the Mediterranean and let the Atlantic burst in through the Gates of Hercules to destroy the evidence.

But Dr. G. Elliot Smith is more conservative. The ingredients of his Heliolithic Theory are gathered plainly enough under the Pharaohs, but the dissemination is by dark ways that lead hither and yon across the world. The low-browed Australians learned magic from the specific concoction invented on the Nile, although it is admitted that many concepts gathered new flavour in India, Cambodia and China before they finally reached America. Dr. Smith's method is admirably illustrated in his *Elephants and Ethnologists* wherein he revives all old identifications of elephants in the art of America and makes new ones. He relates these supposed representations to Buddhist pictures, also dilating on certain grotesque, composite figures of southern Asia which he holds to be the first parents of all American monsters.

Even the most casual reader must realize that the romantic theories outlined above cannot all be true because they oppose each other and fall into riotous discord. Many are flights of childish adventure. Others, sincere and hard-working enough, are based upon the narrow and depressing concept that man in general cannot think for himself but must imitate and remember the actions of a favoured race. The romantic school that decries independent invention is itself stuffed with invention. The argument is consistent only in that it is always made on the curiosæ rather than on the solid achievements of mankind. We now turn to a brief statement of the arguments used by the humble majority of anthropologists where the essential independence of several great civilizations is under discussion.

AMERICAN CIVILIZATION IN AN INDEPENDENT FAMILY

That America was the home of a family of civilizations independent of the family of civilizations in the Old World in all the higher reaches of achievement is the contention of prosaic anthropologists. If this contention is correct then such parallels as do occur on various planes of culture have a tremendous bearing on the innate potentialities of mankind, and thus, in turn, on the future course of political and social evolution.

Mankind is now believed to represent one species of animal subdivided into races. The origin of man himself and the primary development of his culture are considered to have taken place in the great continental masses of Asia, Europe and Africa and there is good evidence that he had reached the general cultural level of the Lower Neolithic before migration out of the Old World continents took place and the species became cosmopolitan. In other words, man was a creature perfected in mind and body, with tools, speech and the rudiments of all important arts before he left home for the ends of the earth.

Civilizations are first of all dependent upon abundant and constant food supply. Without such food supply population cannot become dense, nor leisure be allowed for the graces of life. But civilizations are also dependent upon the creation of loyalties and inhibitions among the members of the social group. The American record indicates in very complete fashion the natural history of civilizations, from the family hunting band type of association up through the fisherman's and farmer's villages to nationalities, including all the members of a language group and even to empires based on conquest and tribute. The psychological bases of leadership—blood, might, wealth and magic—all are found in varying degree, in different parts of America. The blood-bond strikes curious parallels to the Old World in such institutions as cross-cousin marriage, totemic or non-totemic clans, etc., but to claim that these parallels mean historical continuity of an ancient pattern is unjustifiable. They may be reiterated answers to the mechanistic problem of making the family continuous. Ethnographic research shows that the higher types of social organization have their centers in areas of good food supply. Social classifications break clean across the linguistic ones in many instances, indicating that culture may rise or fall quickly and is not necessarily permanent.

The culture areas of American ethnologists rest on a static concept. They correspond to the nuclear distributions of dominant arts on a given horizon or historical level. To some extent they also correspond to environmental provinces, but it is recognized that life may be developed along different lines in the same environmental province, witness the nomadic Apache and the sedentary Pueblo of desert southwestern states. But human culture is dynamic, and if the vertical or historical changes are correlated with the horizontal or geographical changes we obtain storm movements. That is, there is a flowing out from a cultural high into a cultural low as on a weather map.

CONVERGENCE AND DIVERGENCE

The doctrine of convergence, or of convergent evolution, has been used to explain striking similarities between the arts of man in different parts of the world and especially as a reply to the argument that such similarities mean historical connections between widely sundered peoples. By definition convergence means that things originally different have become the same and by divergence that things originally the same have become different. In other words, the proof of historical continuity should be sought in divergence, while convergence in human arts means that some mechanical control affects the object.

These terms, convergence and divergence, are as applicable in nature as in human history and the paleontologist, the botanist, etc., constantly use them. Outside of man convergence is generally explained by a constant environmental or mechanical factor, or set of factors, acting upon different things and slowly transforming them. The same explanation will serve in the case of man because human sensory organs are machines that select for quality. Also similarities in art are apt to arise independently because structure, as in textiles, acts as a limit upon design. In other words selection is controlled both in and out of man's body. The general history of the modification of tools, of designs, etc., show that these are refined and specialized in much the same way as animals and plants in natural evolution.

Similarities in the patterns of social organization, in ceremonial procedure, in mechanical construction, in decorative design etc., are all susceptible to convergences and therefore cannot be

[65]

used without support to argue historical contact between widely separated
peoples, especially if we proceed on
the theory that men are approximately
equal in the matter of the mental and
bodily machine and that they all had an
approximately even start on the Neolithic plane of culture.

Problems of cultural interrelations
on the civilized plane between the
Eastern and Western hemispheres
must be decided on basic arguments,
not on merely curious similarities. The
points used in the notorious Heliolithic
Theory of Smith and Perry are mostly
curiosæ without really important relations to the matters of social life.
Agriculture, dealing with an entirely
different set of domesticated plants in
America than it does in Asia, Africa
and Europe, more than offsets the couvade and other strange resemblances.
Pottery, weaving and metal working in
the archæology of America rise from a
low to a high plane within spaces of

time that can be accurately measured and fixed in a system of world chronology.

COMPARISONS OF AMERICAN AND OLD WORLD AGRICULTURE

Two principal places of origin of agriculture and domestic animals can be distinguished in the Old World and two more in the New World, as well as a number of secondary centres established in much later times. Of the two focal points in each hemisphere the older in each case corresponds to an arid tropical or subtropical environment and the younger to a humid environment well within the tropics. The basic civilizations rising out of assured supplies of food may be classified as:

1. *The Civilization of Wheat,* with its centre in Mesopotamia and the Nile Valley and its principal extension eastward over northern India, the Tarim

Basin, and the plains of China. The adjustment of wheat to the Persian highlands and to Europe came long after cultivation in the low hot valleys. In the food complex of this civilization we find wheat, barley, lentils, peas, grapes, etc., with cattle, sheep, and goats coming into use as sources of meat, milk and butter. Rye, oats, cabbages, etc., were comparatively late domestications on the northern fringe.

2. *The Civilization of Maize,* with its original centre on the rather arid highlands of Central America. In this complex we find a strong vegetarian diet with maize, beans and squashes occupying first place. Domesticated animals were few and relatively unimportant in the dietary; turkeys may be mentioned. The two arid land agricultural complexes have no factor in common, plants in the two sets not being even remotely similar. That of the Old World may be dated tentatively as beginning about 5000 B.C. on the evi-

dence of recent explorations near the
Red Sea, while the New World civilization may be somewhat younger in
spite of the fact that the American
plants in general are more highly
domesticated than those of Asia (*i.e.,*
carried farther from the wild types and
adapted to a wider climatic range).

3. *The Civilization of Rice.* The
locus of this civilization was the humid
area of southern China, Indonesia, and
Bengal in India. In addition to rice,
other important plants were yams,
breadfruit, bananas and coconuts.
Pigs and chickens also appear to have
been domesticated here.

4. *The Civilization of Manioc.* The
corresponding civilization of the wet
tropics in America, inaugurated by the
Mayas, before 600 B.C. according to the
evidence of their calendar, was in considerable part supported by maize,
beans, squashes, etc., modified to meet
humid conditions. But a number of
wet land plants were domesticated, in-

cluding cacao, sweet potatoes, and the manioc root which furnishes tapioca and cassava. The best lowland culture of South America flourished near the mouth of the Amazon, and this appears to have been the original home of several domesticated plants, including manioc. In both the Old and New Worlds the humid type civilizations did not get under way till about the time of Christ, with the first indications of culture 500-1000 years earlier.

As regards food plants it has already been stated that the combined botanical, archæological and historical evidence discloses no food plants common to both the Old and New Worlds. It is true that the botanical evidence indicates that the coconut belongs to a family nearly all of whose members are American, nevertheless it is very certain that the domesticated coconut was unknown here and that it was known in the Old World. Some cases may appear doubtful if all opinions must be

[70]

given equal weight. Thus some persons, finding sweet potatoes widely spread in China, the Philippines, New Zealand, etc., have naively considered them native of these parts. But in the Philippines at least these roots still bear the Aztec name, camote, while yams were introduced into America under the African name. One may find statements that the banana existed in America but the native names for it are nearly all variants of the Spanish platano and the record of introduction is precise enough.

Indeed only one species of cultivated plant appears to have been cosmopolitan at the time of the discovery of America, namely the common gourd, well equipped to float its way around the world. As for cotton, the wild species have blown around the world and are found on oceanic islands. Three species in America and two in the Old World have been reduced to cultivation. The Old World species

are decidedly inferior. Also the archæological specimens of American cotton
are much older than those of Assyria,
India or China.

In connection with American agriculture there are some extremely in-
teresting problems in the genetics of
plants. Archæology is able to restore
the lines of migration for domesticated
plants in America and the sequence of
climatic adjustments. This is important because some of these plants, for
example maize, have wider adjustments
than the domesticated plants of the Old
World. In the Pueblo area the lowest
culture level shows a single type of
maize of the flint variety. In upper
levels we get flour corn of different
colors, beans, squashes, cotton, etc.

CERAMIC AND TEXTILE ARTS

The coordination in distribution
between ceramic art and agriculture is
quite exact in America if we omit the

unbaked blood-cemented pottery of the Eskimos. Some marginal tribes like the Mandan and the Huron probably received pottery as part of the agricultural complex. Nevertheless we must also recognize that pottery is naturally an art of sedentary peoples which is of slight service to nomadic peoples. Some of the western Algonquin tribes on passing out of the agricultural area used pottery to a slight extent and then gave it up. Although records of pottery manufacture exist for the Shoshone and some other tribes of the Basin Area who had winter homes in the valleys and summer camps on the hills, it never was important among them. Similarly there is a discontinuance of pottery in South America when we leave the limits of agriculture, except for a marginal zone of sporadic cases.

Pottery art delimits special cultures by its full and permanent record of decorative art. Frequently it is found in stratified deposits which furnish evidence of historical sequence. It may give proofs of the interchange of mechanical ideas between culture areas. An example of this develops from the distribution of the tripod support which is a common character of pottery from Colombia to central Mexico, but is seldom met with in Peru and never met with in the Pueblo area. Another example is the process of negative painting after the fashion of the batik, the design being put on with wax before the sizing colors are applied. This process began in late Archaic pottery in Mexico and extended as far as Peru. The shapes of the objects decorated by this process and the designs used were local while the process was widely distributed.

The potter's wheel, known to the earliest Egyptians, was never invented in America but for that matter neither was the wheel in any of its other mechanical uses known in the New World.

Glazing of a kind was used to a limited extent. First there was a kind of self-glazing pottery manufactured in Salvador and southern Guatemala from a clay which suffused under fire owing to the presence of lead. Second there was a true glaze paint used by the Pueblo tribes of New Mexico, the basis of which was galena. Colors on the warm register, especially reds, were widely used for sizing and also for painted designs, being mostly founded on the oxides of iron. In Costa Rica there was a local use of manganese to make a lustrous brown-purple. Light bluish color, possibly from the purpura shell fish, a species of Murex, is also used here to a very slight extent. But aside from this the only cold-register paints are found in the Nasca and Ica pottery of Peru. Here the purplish blue is of unknown origin.

Convergences in textile art of the Old and New Worlds are seen in machines, form of weaving and designs. The controlling factors are clearly discernible and explanations of the independent inventions and the numerous convergences are not far to seek. While the first immigrants to America doubtless had mats and basketry and knew how to twist string, it is not likely that they were acquainted with flexible weaving. At least it is pretty certain that the loom and spindle whorl were invented independently in America. Also several fiber plants were domesticated and several splendid dyes brought into use. If it is impossible for a stream to rise higher than its source, how can persons who wish to derive all worthwhile American achievements from the Old World explain the wonderful perfection of the textile art in Peru? For in variety of construction, fineness of weave and brilliancy of coloring Peruvian textile products are without rival anywhere.

The warp-weighted loom—if indeed this clumsy machine deserves the name of loom—does occur on both sides of the North Pacific among the Ainu of Japan and the Chilcat of Alaska. If the Scandinavians brought looms to Greenland they were doubtless of this type. But there is no suspicion of the warp-weighted loom in Mexico and Peru. The true loom principle emerges from basketry manipulation when some sort of harness is devised to move a whole set of warp threads in a single act—that is, when a shed is produced. In America the loom—with warp beams, harness, comb and batten sword—was distributed from Colorado to Argentine, following closely the distribution of cotton cultivation.

Practically all kinds of cloth were developed in America, plain weaving, twilling, tapestry, brocade, gauze, double cloth, etc. Also we find designs applied in a great many different ways, among which tie-dying in the warp and in the finished cloth may be mentioned. As regards dyes we have

American indigo, distinct from Asiatic indigo, also the cochineal insect which was domesticated, and a purple dye drawn from a species of Murex. Here is a nice example of the independent seizing of similar resources in nature. The American Murex differs in species from the Mediterranean and Indian ones, and could not have been transported.

THE METAL AGES DO NOT APPLY
IN AMERICA

Another basic comparison between the civilizations of the two hemispheres can be made on metals. In Old World archeology we have bronze and iron giving their names to well defined levels of human culture with the likelihood that some usage of gold and of native copper preceded the true Age of Bronze. This age may begin as early as 3200 B.C., while iron came into fairly common use about 800 B.C.

Metals are unduly emphasized during the grandiose stages of civilization in Egypt, Assyria and China and the use of bronze strikes a cultural horizon from Ireland to Japan.

In the New World, on the other hand, there was probably no very ancient use of metals, but several independent areas in which a late and partial use must be noted. Native copper was hammered in shape for tools, etc. in regions adjacent to supply, as in southern Alaska, along the Coppermine River, in northern Canada, and in Victoria Land. In the area south of the Great Lakes there was a similar use not only of native copper, but also of gold, native silver and some meteoric iron. Although the Mound-builders made excellent repousée designs on sheets of hammered copper, they never learned the art of smelting ore or casting molten metals.

In South America, the West Indies, Central America and Mexico the knowledge of metals was practically continuous except over the South American lowlands and those parts of Argentine and Chile lying beyond the influence of the Peruvian civilization. In the West Indies the gold apparently came from local sources in Porto Rico and Santo Domingo. Perhaps metal art among the Arawacks was derived from the mainland of Venezuela where rare specimens are found. For the rest of the great area boasting metal work we can draw a line as regards technique across southern Colombia. North of this is found the pseudo-filigrane method of casting from wax models built up in thread-like details. This process was used over Colombia, Panama, etc., to Mexico. South of the division line, in Equador and Peru, the pseudo-filigrane technique is not apparent, although the lost-wax process was known. The finest pieces of Equadorian and Peruvian metal work are ornamented with repousée.

On both sides of the technical dividing line we find a common knowledge of gold, silver, copper and various alloys. Tin and copper were mixed to make bronze, but no definite formula seems to have been reached. Platinum was used in western Colombia and Equador, and lead was pretty certainly known in Mexico.

Now although the evidence is very clear that metal working came into Mexico from the south, it is also just as certain that there was no knowledge of it in the Maya area at the time of the First Empire, the dated monuments of which run from about 100 B.C. to about 630 A.D. No specimens of metal and no metal stains have been observed at Copan, Quirigua, etc., nor are metal objects represented on the early Maya sculptures as details of the dress, although shells and jade objects are clearly drawn. The ruin of Las Quebradas, belonging to the same age as Quirigua, is situated upon the richest placer mine in Guatemala. Although most of this site has been excavated and many pieces of pottery and jade recovered, not one specimen of worked metal has come to light.

Under the Toltec kings, Huetzin, Ihuitimal and Quetzalcoatl, tribute in metals was collected in Guatemala. Most of the gold sacrificed in the Sacred Cenote at Chichen Itza in Yucatan during this, the Toltec period, was imported from Costa Rica and Panama and some came from as far away as the middle Cauca valley. From these facts we may conclude that the metal age in Central America and Mexico began between 600 and 1100 A.D.

THE CALENDAR

A considerable number of papers bearing on possible relations between the civilizations of the New and Old Worlds attempt to draw parallels in the systems of counting time and argue derivation of the Central American calendar from Chinese zodiacs, etc. Of course time-counts must take notice of facts in nature. The zodiac, as the path of the planets, is an observable thing, as is the length of the month or year. Time observations of some kind or other are universal.

Natural calendars of the sidereal year type, without months, are apparently the lowest, existing in Australia, South Africa and the South American lowlands. In this type the heliacal rising of constellations in correspondence with the seasons is noted. Next follows the type with twelve months in a year, or thirteen when necessary. This luni-solar calendar is found pretty widely over the world—in parts of Africa, practically all of Asia and Europe as well as North America. Mathematical calendars where the month becomes a more or less formal part of the year come in with high civilization, very often on the formula $12 \times 30 + 5 = 365$.

The Central American calendar is built on a system that finds no parallel in the Old World. It is $18 \times 20 + 5$ combined with a permutation of $13 \times 20 = 260$. The dates are the number of elapsed days from a mundane era which equals October 14, 3373 B.C. in the backward projection of our present Gregorian calendar. The time-count began to function on August 6, 613 B.C. The writing out of the Maya calendar involved place-value a thousand years before it was known anywhere in the Old World and an eral count of days 300 years before the first eral count of years in the Old World (The Era of the Seleucidæ, October 1, 312 B.C.). In other words, an analysis of the science of ancient America shows products of high originality and this fact relieves us from the necessity of explaining intellectually and artistically advanced features of New World civilizations by diffusion from Europe or Asia.

The conformity of natural time cycles which the Greeks reached in the Cycle of Meton was 19 years = 235 months = 6940 days. This is reached by the Mayas as 1 Katun (7200 days) minus 1 Tzolkin (260 days) = 6940 days. The Egyptian Sothic Cycle is an attempt at a natural cycle reached in marvelous fashion by the Mayas. The Egyptian Sothic Cycle is 1461 × 365 = 1460 × 365.25, that is 1461 calendarical years equal 1460 years according to the Julian formula. But here the Nile flooded in accordance with the tropical year and the dog star rose in accordance with the sidereal year. These elements are really incompatible, the error being about 12 days in one cycle. In the Mayan arrangement, 29 permutation rounds of 52 calendarical years each equal 1507 tropical years. The error here is a small fraction of a day. The Mayan

calculations on eclipses, planetary rev-
elations and tropical years are mar-
velously accurate and are expressed in
a peculiar kind of mathematics associ-
ated with a peculiar kind of hiero-
glyphs.

The time-counts of Central America
give a shaft of accurate chronology in
the centre of the New World and by
taking note of trade specimens and link-
ing features in decorative arts, ceremonies, etc., we can establish far-reach-
ing horizons in archeology.

DISEASES

Diseases caused by parasites invad-
ing the human body have local origins
and are distributed by man himself.
The chance that the same parasitical
ailment might originate spontaneously
in different areas is negligible. Of
course the organisms of disease are
vastly older than man. The human
host may be the last of a series of hosts

[86]

for the parasite. Nevertheless the historical record pretty clearly shows that disturbances of this sort have a continuous history of dissemination from an original pathological adaptation to man. Since the conditions of the body vary but slightly according to climates the pathological agents tend to become cosmopolitan.

Parasitic diseases could hardly maintain themselves among men without reasonably dense populations. We may assume that the men coming into America were free from most if not all such diseases. After the independent inventions of agriculture some kinds of disease arose in America and others in the Old World, both in regions of concentrated population, made possible by the improvement in food supply.

The principal New World diseases were yellow fever and syphilis, the former practically limited to the humid tropics and the latter more widely spread over highlands as well as lowlands among nearly all the agricultural populations of America. The story of the dissemination of this latter affection over the rest of the world began with the return of Columbus and ended with the discovery of the last island groups in the Pacific. It was the introduction of this ailment to the Hawaiian Islanders by the sailors of Captain Cook that led to the murder of that gallant explorer on his return from Alaska.

The introduction of small-pox, measles, typhoid, cholera, etc., into America is fully authenticated. It does not appear that a single important disease of parasitic type was common to the New and Old Worlds at the time of the discovery of America and its colonization by Europeans.

OTHER COMPARISONS

It would be possible to go much farther in these comparisons, for re-

markable similarities and differences—
the former no more significant than
the latter—exist between the intellectual structures of man in the two hemispheres. There is the independent development of priestcraft and statecraft
devoted to a more plastic material than
potter's clay, namely the group mind
of any and every society of human beings. There are the parallelisms and
divergences in all the arts, including
graphic and plastic decoration and
representation, music, dancing, and the
prosaic and poetical use of words.
Then there are numerous cases of adaptation and invention which contribute
to the proofs of inventive genius among
ancient Americans. There is the preparation of bark cloth and paper, and
the preparation of rubber from the
coagulated latex of the Castilla elastica.
This substance was made into balls for
a special game. It was also used to tip
drum sticks, to make capes and other
parts of dress impervious to water, etc.

Then there was the burning of lime-stone to make a mortar for architectural purposes, and there was even a use of brick and tiles. These are all parallel to developments in the Old World but with a factor of originality.

But there are also notable absences. For instance, the wheel as a mechanical device appears nowhere in the New World. Even an imperfect correlation emphasizes the inventiveness of man and supports the logical position that the ancient Americans achieved by far the greater portion of their culture in the New World without occult help from the dominant civilization of the Old World.

And yet it is apparent that man did reach the New World from the Old. He did this, according to the prosaic anthropologist, not by crossing the broad Atlantic and the still broader Pacific but by taking advantage of an ancient land bridge between the continents which likewise served as a high-

way for other animals. This land
bridge extended from Siberia to
Alaska and at the present time is
sunken less than 100 feet below the sea.
But there was a still more ancient land
bridge across the North Atlantic which
may have served for the precursors of
man.

EARLY MAN IN AMERICA

We are accustomed to think of the
Old World as the place of origin for
the primates, the highest order of life,
and the order leading to man. The ac-
cumulating data on the Eocene fauna
of New Mexico, Wyoming and other
western states indicate that the home
of the primates may have been in
North America and that such primitive lemuroids as the Notharctidæ in
middle Eocene age rose out of such
primitive insectivores as Nothodectes
in the lower Eocene, or Paleocene as it
is sometimes called. The Tarsius

group under Lemuroidiæ is also found in America and this is supposed by paleontologists to be near the direct line of man's development. The Notharctidæ of the New World are tied into the available paleontological record in a better way than the contemporary Adapidæ of Europe.

In this connection it should be kept in mind that the extent of Eocene land in North America was much greater than in Europe. The North Atlantic land-bridge across Labrador, Greenland, Iceland, the Faroes, etc., was then above water serving as a highway for land animals between the two hemispheres under favorable climatic conditions. It now lies below a shallow sea. Also Europe at that time was cut off by wide water masses from Asia and Africa. In other words North America and Western Europe were parts of one continent.

The present American monkeys are higher than the lemuroids of either hemisphere and may have arisen out of the Notharctidæ. There is a break in the paleontological record in America from Eocene to Pliocene or Pleistocene and if the present American monkeys are not considered descendants of the geologically early forms then we must imagine an invasion from Asia via the Siberia-Alaskan bridge because the North Atlantic isthmus was submerged before the Miocene.

If the single tooth from a late Pliocene formation in Nebraska, assigned to a large anthropoid called Hesperopithicus, is vindicated as belonging to an upper primate we may have a real problem of the anthropoidal precursors of man for America. Previous to the finding of this tooth evidence of anthropoid apes and of archaic types of man was wanting in America. Various animals contemporary with archaic man found their way into America from Asia.

Nevertheless nearly a century of

search has failed to furnish satisfactory
proof of man in America before or
during the last advance of the glaciers,
and the weight of evidence now lies
heavily against the assumption that
paleolithic man was, in fact, present.
An examination of the most primitive
marginal types of Indian culture discloses the smooth stone celt and other
characteristic products of the Neolithic
period. Indeed it appears that the
final dissemination of man beyond the
limits of the Old World cluster of continents took place on this horizon, since
the Australian likewise has smooth
stone implements. The most primitive
tribes of the world seem to be safely
Neolithic, but on the nomadic-hunting
rather than the sedentary-agricultural
stage.

Man probably entered America on
the early Neolithic horizon before the
invention of agriculture or the domestication of any animal except possibly
the dog. The earliest possible date of

his coming would depend on the retreat of the ice sheet from the road
leading to the Siberia-Alaskan land
bridge. It is believed that the glacial
stages were roughly contemporaneous
for all parts of the Arctic continental
mass, yet criteria of age relating to
the advent of man into America are of
the vaguest sort. The archæological
record in Mexico and Central America can hardly be pushed back beyond
3000-4000 B.C. for sedentary culture.
Before this date and after the retreat
of the ice are some ten thousand or
more years.

The present differentiation in language and physical type among American Indians is supposed to be sufficient
to cover a large part of this interval.
The difficulty here is that the original
stream of immigration was doubtless
already mixed. Of course it is perfectly obvious that some correlation
expressing the gist of history must be
effected in America between the

present incompatible classifications of culture, language and physical type.

Properly speaking, language is a social convention and therefore a part of culture. It seems to be by far the most persistent part since the evidence indicates that the sundered members of the Athabascan stock, for instance, have but a small ingredient of common usage outside the forms of speech. Obviously the Aztecs and the Shoshone at opposite ends of the area occupied by the Uto-Aztecan stock, and at opposite ends of the social scale, must be brought into an original conformity, and the same problem remains for other far-flung language groups.

Physical anthropology has demonstrated the absence of archaic types of man in the known American record and it has demonstrated that there is considerable fluctuation about a normal race standard. But it has not demonstrated a concordance at any stage with language. To say that physical classifications of American Indians cannot be correlated with cultural and linguistic classifications is merely to insist that physical characters are mobile and without value as historical criteria, except possibly in large averages. It is absurd for physical anthropologists to insist, in extenuation of their failure, that linguistic evidences of social unity can be neglected on the grounds that a physical entity in population may lose its language and other elements of culture. It would not lose these without some marks of the struggle and without some mixture of blood with the conqueror.

CONCLUSION

From all points of view, then, it appears there are no sound reasons for the interpretation of history demanded by the romantic school in the science that studies the origin of man and his institutions. It is safe to file a general demurrer against mummification, the couvade, helioliths, lost continents, African jargon, elephant trunks and all the other sensational arguments which have formed the basis for theories of occult migrations and forgotten conquests. One might as well have distribution of culture by telepathy and intellectual osmosis. The one real opportunity that Europe had to influence America was when the Norsemen lived for 400 years in Greenland: yet no evidence of influences emanating from them have been found even among the neighbouring Eskimos. What likelihood, then, is there of the Phœnician galleys or Chinese junks having planted the seed of civilization in Mexico or Peru?

THE
DIFFUSION CONTROVERSY

By Alexander Goldenweiser
*Lecturer on Anthropology at the New School of
Social Research, New York*

Differences in scientific views are
wholesome. In a problem such as the
diffusion of culture, with its many theoretical tangles and objective com-
plexities, differences in point of view
are not only pardonable but inevitable
and necessary. Unfortunately, however, the gladiatorial combat suffers
both from misrepresentation of the
views of opponents and from lack of
clarity as to the real issues at hand.

When Professor Elliot Smith writes
that "the theory maintained by the vast
majority of anthropologists to-day is
that in any community civilization can
and did grow up and develop quite

independently of similar events happening elsewhere in the world," one may well ask for the names of the anthropologists who constitute this "vast majority." Being one of the tribe myself, after a fashion, I experience difficulty in mentioning even a *single* anthropologist who holds such a view. All but the most dogmatic of the old-time evolutionists would have hesitated to exclude "all considerations of contact or prompting directly or indirectly" when similarities in beliefs and customs among different peoples are concerned. Tylor, for example, went out of his way repeatedly to repudiate such an attitude, to say nothing of modern ethnologists, including the "vast majority" of Americanists, to whom the tracing of culture contacts is ever of uppermost concern.

Again, when the famous anatomist writes: "It is utterly unjustifiable to assume, as modern ethnological theories implicitly do, that human behaviour was totally different before writing was devised. There is not a scrap of evidence to suggest that our unliterary predecessors had a remarkable aptitude for invention far transcending that of modern man. Nor again is there anything to justify the even more reckless assumption that this imaginary aptitude found expression in a stereotyped form in every place where ancient civilization developed," against whom is this broadside directed? Surely not against American anthropologists, nor, for that matter, *any anthropologist of any account anywhere in the scientific world to-day.* For no such fabulous aptitude for invention is attributed to primitive man by any modern student of the subject; ethnologists assume most emphatically that human behaviour in primitive times was much the same as it is to-day; as to the "stereotyped form" in which "ancient civilization developed," no one could outdo the modern ethnologist in his zeal to point out and appreciate the kaleidoscopic variety of patterns assumed by civilization in early days.

Having paved the way for the presentation of his theory in this questionable fashion, Professor Smith devotes the rest of his essay to citing attested instances of diffusion. But here also one cannot but feel that his efforts are being wasted. For no one doubts the *reality* of diffusion nor its importance in the building up of culture complexes.

Thus we reach the end of the author's study without reading one word about the real issues: Is there such a thing as independent invention? And, if so, is it frequent or exceptional? Also: is it always easy or even possible to determine whether similar customs or beliefs in two or more places are to be attributed to independent development or to the operation of diffusion in the course of historic contact?

In his reflections upon "The Life of Culture" Dr. Malinowski raises the discussion to a higher level of fairness and realism. We believe with him that "in the case of every modern invention, we know that it is invariably made and remade time after time in different places, by different men along slightly different roads, independently of one another," and accept with him the truth that "every cultural achievement is due to a process or growth in which diffusion and invention have equal shares." We share Dr. Malinowski's repudiation of a purely mechanical view of diffusion as a mere transfer of this or that from one place to another, and heartily endorse his insistence on the much more complicated nature of the facts of adoption and adaptation of cultural features. Dr. Malinowski is emphatically right in stressing the significance of biological and psychological factors which express themselves in similar urges and wants, and inevitably lead to similar solutions, at least in man's initial adjustments to nature and to culture.

On the other hand, when the author declares that "culture is not contagious," that "it has neither been invented nor diffused, but imposed by the natural conditions which drive man upon the path of progress with inexorable determinism," our sympathy is no longer aroused. For natural conditions do not drive man anywhere except to the extent that he must meet them; moreover, what is "the path of progress" and is it a path of *progress, always?* And where is the evidence for an "inexorable determinism"? Nor are we illumined when reading that "the remedy for anthropology lies not in conjuring up one conjecture in the place of another, but in giving the Science of Man a foundation of real fact open to observation, in making it bear upon the practical and vital issues of the day." Facts as such will not settle the issues before us—are not facts "scarcest raw material"?—for the problem is one of interpretation and analysis; nor is it at all clear by what magic the theoretical issues of diffusion and independent invention can be made to bear "upon the practical and vital issues of to-day," nor why the "remedy for anthropology" should be sought in this direction.

Instead, it should have been made clear—as neither of the authors has done—that the study of children and the analysis of cultural situations where the facts and processes are *known,* bring irrefutable evidence of man's creativeness or inventive capacity; that cultural diffusion and adaptation are as omnipresent and significant as invention; that there are instances of cultural similarities of such complexity (as would be, for example, a Gothic cathedral in Australia) that diffusion can be decided upon without hesitation; that in other instances, where a cultural feature is relatively simple and widespread (such as animism), repeated independent invention is equally obvious; that in an enormous number of cases, on the other hand, no such facile decision is possible; and that it is here that careful analysis and a thorough estimate of geographical and historical probability and evidence must be called into consultation. Also, when all this is done, a sufficiently large number of cases will remain where no safe or even tentative conclusion can be reached as between diffusion and independent invention. And, in honesty and fairness, this also must be admitted.

PSYCHE

AN ILLUSTRATED QUARTERLY REVIEW OF GENERAL AND APPLIED PSYCHOLOGY

Edited by C. K. OGDEN

Editor of "The International Library of Psychology, Philosophy, and Scientific Method," and "The New Science Series."

RECENT CONTRIBUTORS INCLUDE:

Bertrand Russell, F.R.S.

$5.00 Postpaid Per Annum

W · W · NORTON & COMPANY, INC.
70 FIFTH AVENUE   NEW YORK